To:

____

je t'aime

MY DREAMS

XOXO

Я люблю тебя

you are
my
sunshine

Mon Amour

For you

you are
the
best

you are
loved

Ti amo

Be
Mine

I love
YOU
. to the .
moon
AND
back

Love

Ich liebe dich

I
love you
more
than all
stars
in the sky

To My Wonderful
Daughter & Husband
Happy Valentine's
Day
Across the
miles!

AFGREKI
EU TE AMO
MILUJI TĚ
Ľúbim t'a
Kocham Ciebie
Ti amo
Aishiteru
T'estimo Je t'aime
Te dua VOLIM TE
Te ubesk
I love you
S'agapo
Mi amas vin Bahibak
Ich liebe dich
M'bi fe

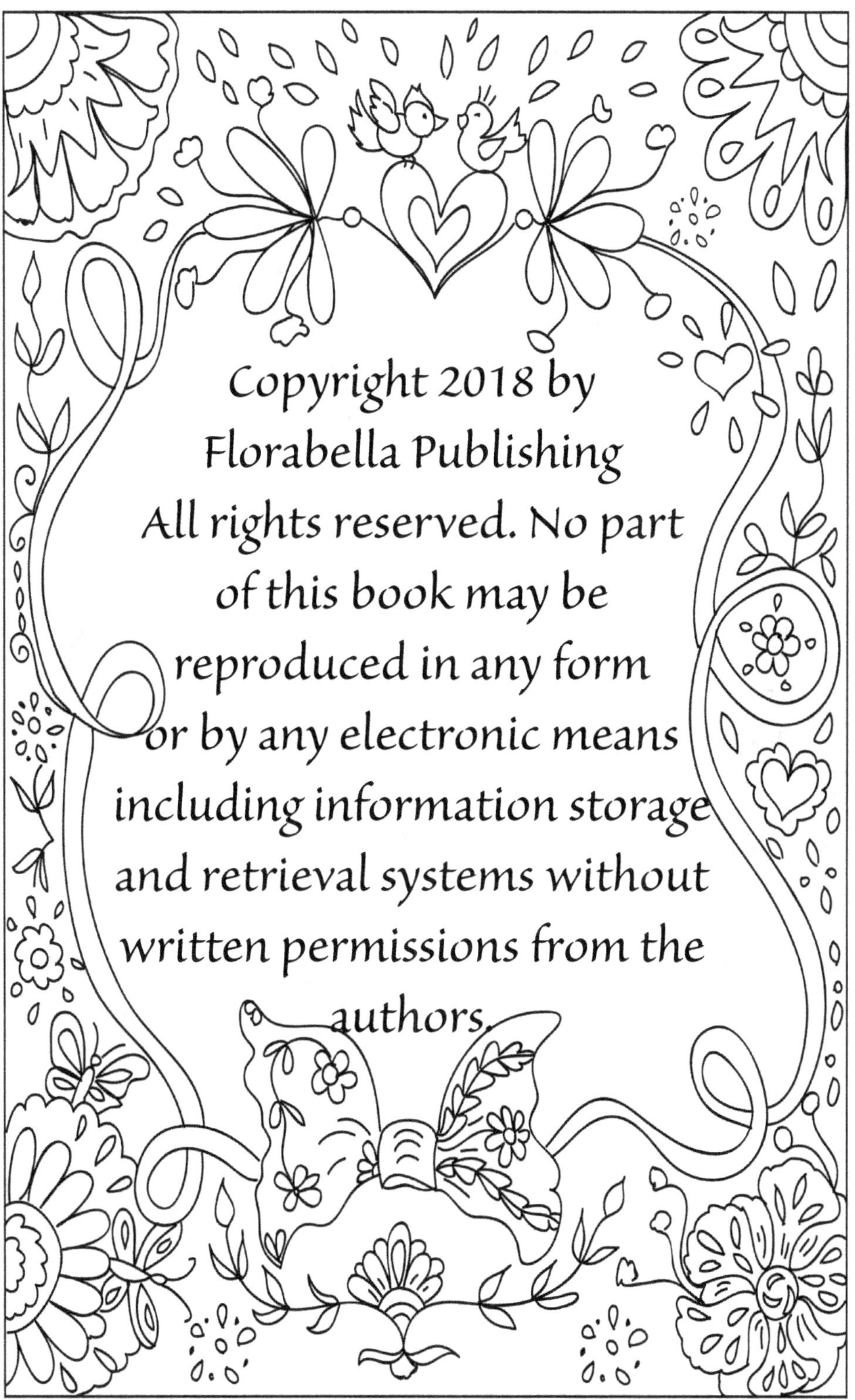
Copyright 2018 by
Florabella Publishing
All rights reserved. No part
of this book may be
reproduced in any form
or by any electronic means
including information storage
and retrieval systems without
written permissions from the
authors.

LOVE
We miss you!
Love,